Activities We Do

We Exercise

by Connor Stratton

FOCUS READERS
SCOUT

www.focusreaders.com

Focus Readers is distributed by North Star Editions:
sales@northstareditions.com | 888-417-0195

Produced for Focus Readers by Red Line Editorial.

Photographs ©: wavebreakmedia/Shutterstock Images, cover, 1; TinnaPong/Shutterstock Images, 4, 16 (top left), 16 (bottom left); Africa Studio/Shutterstock Images, 7 (top); Spotmatik Ltd/Shutterstock Images, 7 (bottom); FatCamera/iStockphoto, 9; Vgstockstudio/Shutterstock Images, 11; RPA Studio/Shutterstock Images, 13 (top); Gregory Johnston/Shutterstock Images, 13 (bottom), 16 (bottom right); FatCamera/iStockphoto, 15; Ruslan Grumble/Shutterstock Images, 16 (top right)

Library of Congress Cataloging-in-Publication Data
Names: Stratton, Connor, author.
Title: We exercise / by Connor Stratton.
Description: Lake Elmo, MN : Focus Readers, 2020. | Series: Activities we do | Includes index. | Audience: K to Grade 3.
Identifiers: LCCN 2018060800 (print) | LCCN 2019000096 (ebook) | ISBN 9781641859929 (PDF) | ISBN 9781641859356 (ebook) | ISBN 9781641857970 (hardcover) | ISBN 9781641858663 (pbk.)
Subjects: LCSH: Exercise--Juvenile literature.
Classification: LCC RA781 (ebook) | LCC RA781 .S869 2020 (print) | DDC 612.7/6--dc23
LC record available at https://lccn.loc.gov/2018060800

Printed in the United States of America
Mankato, MN
May, 2019

About the Author

Connor Stratton loves ice-skating, eating popcorn, and watching movies with friends. He lives in Minnesota.

Table of Contents

arm
leg

Exercise Is Fun

We like to exercise.

We move our **arms**.

We move our **legs**.

We exercise with friends.

We exercise with family.

It is good for our health.

Sports and Play

We play sports.

We run with the ball.

ball

We play outside.

We jump **rope**.

rope

Using Our Bodies

We move our bodies.

Our breath gets fast.

Our hearts beat fast.

Our skin gets **sweaty**.

sweat

We are tired.

Our exercise is over.

We had fun.

Glossary

arms

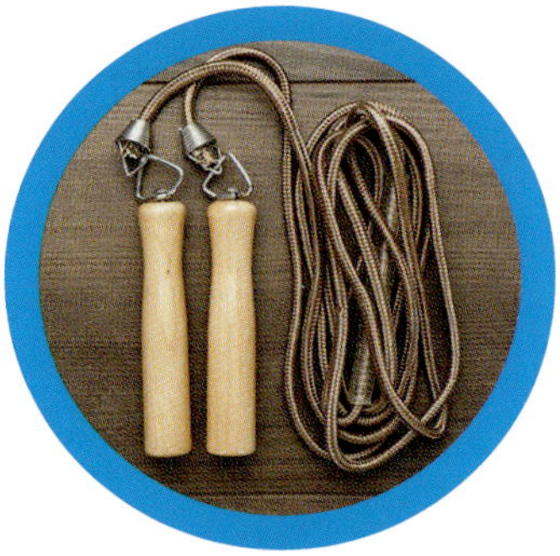

rope

legs

sweaty

Index